Inspirations
of
Creativity

Quotes from *Conquering the Chaos of Creativity*

by Doug Patton

Author services by Pedernales Publishing, LLC
www.pedernalespublish.com
ISBN 978-1-7360811-6-7 Paperback Edition
       978-1-7360811-7-4 Hardcover Edition
       978-1-7360811-8-1 Digital Edition

Library of Congress Control Number: 2023901497
Printed in the United States of America

To my daughter, Heather and son, Sean
You are my inspiration

CONTENTS

The Seven Foundations of Creativity

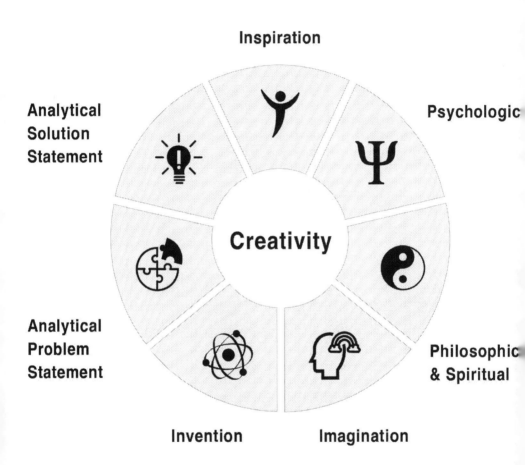

The connected and interactive
foundations of creativity

M y landmark book about creative problem-solving, *Conquering the Chaos of Creativity*, is the genesis of this volume, which contains quotes to inspire and nurture creationists' journey to find truth. With this book, I have created an imaginative environment in which I invite you to explore and expand your intuitive potential.

The chaos of creativity is a free space uncontrolled by language, knowledge, and social limitations. It is an emancipated zone of intellectual, spiritual, and emotional freedom you can use to build an empowered creative construct that is uniquely yours. May these quotes inspire your thoughts, energize your creativity, and courageously empower your mind to imagine more.

Chaos of creativity - The home of all creativity and imagination in a universe of total freedom with no boundaries. A powerful place that allows you to convene spiritual and intellectual nurturing for the genesis of revolutionary constructs of creativity.

As is the case with life, the path to conquer the chaos of creativity is a journey, not a destination. Creativity is a beautiful and unique world you can explore; this is your chance to imagine more.

The chaos of creativity is a place of freedom
where you can create a personal
dynamic construct that enables you to search
for the courage, vision, and strength needed to
empower your innate idealism.

Creativity is an alarm clock that awakens you
to the catalyst of change.

Creativity compass - A navigation tool providing guidance in the process of exploring creative chaos

The creativity compass helps those who have gotten lost in the chaos of self-discovery and must navigate it to find their creative truth.

With the knowledge needed to break all barriers to creativity, you can boldly explore your unlimited imagination.

When we embrace the totality of spirit, soul, mind, emotion, and physicality, the heart of creativity is empowered, connecting us to the unlimited power of our imagination.

Creativity is an interactive construct of imagination that can enable an original dialectic of cultural creative linguistics capable of empowering revolutionary discovery.

Inspiration Creativity

Connecting with your passion can catalyze revolutionary change. The journey to find your intrinsic idealism is fueled by your inspired belief. This inspiration is the genesis of creativity and imagination that must be cherished.

Any confinement in your life, whether self-imposed or exerted by an outside force, cannot be diminished by the bright light of your burgeoning passion.

Immersing yourself in the solution process of discovery is the key to creativity.

View the world through the looking glass of the problem you are solving; everything you see, hear, feel, and experience is part of the solution.

Immersion awareness - A creative technique that allows you to become completely immersed in the entirety of what you experience as part of your exploration of new ideas. Everything you see, feel, hear, and think becomes a new inspirational solution.
Just as you dive into a pool, physically immersing your body and mind, so too do you use this process of inspirational immersion to immerse your mind.

Immersion awareness is the process of dreaming about, expressing, and associating with new possible ideas that enables your mind to look beyond what you currently perceive and envision new realities.

Immersion allows us to view everything in our environment as a potential solution for our complex thoughts and dreams. It reveals that inspiration is all around us; it is everywhere and in everything.

Because I believed in what I was doing, exhaustion did not affect me. Belief unlocks tremendous potential within you.

You fight a most courageous battle by
valuing awareness more than pain and fear.
I have fought it my entire life with every breath
I have, fortifying belief with more belief.

Every conceptual thought has humanity
and energy.

In the instant of inspiration, we are healed,
elevated, and conceived anew.

Pain, injury, frustration, and self-doubt are the
seeds of great revolutionary thought.
The ability one develops in overcoming mental
injury creates a construct that can be applied
to become a powerful creative
problem-solving force.

It is important to realize that there is a
capability inside of you more powerful
than any obstacle.

The act of finding your passion and belief is
one of the most powerful forces in creativity.

The future of innovation and creative revolution belongs to those who believe in their idealistic dreams and have the faith needed to follow them.

When you believe what you are working on is the most important thing in the world, you unlock your vast potential, opening the door to revolutionary change.

Inventing is an act of humility that involves reverence and respect for any problem you are solving. You must commit all your heart, spirit, and soul.

There are no unimportant projects—only uninspired designers.

Freedom of thought, with the willingness to express it, is possibly the most treasured aspect of creativity.

You must wish to attain creative freedom with the most passionate desire possible.

Creativity, imagination, and freedom must be cherished, protected, and empowered.

Believing in the creativity of your inspired dreams enables you to break free from the prison of thought. Follow your biggest and most broad dream. When you know you are right, there is no raging river of creativity that can drown you.

The only guiding light in the creative darkness is the knowledge that you are right.
This knowledge is based upon the power and accuracy of the creative tools and methodology you have developed.

The journey of creativity contains battles in which you cannot be meek; you must be resolute in attitude and focus.

Conquering the chaos of creativity requires a highly enthusiastic and energized state of mind—an unstoppable force of nature.

It is time to wake up, act courageously, and energize your sense of purpose. Within you is a force capable of much more than just solving problems. When channeled, it can transform the essence of who you are. Will you choose to wake up or to remain asleep?

The bright light of creativity is lit by your passionate pursuit of idealism, awakening you in the darkness of your visionary slumber.

When lost in the slumber of the status quo, it is essential to quickly wake up, embracing the energy of creative change.

Work to understand yourself, practice to become aware of your vast potential, and empower your own creative construct to conquer the chaos of creativity.

Inherently, you have powerful momentum that can wake up your mind and break you out of the state of stasis that has held your creativity captive.

Psychological
Creativity

When harnessed, the innate process of the mind renews and energizes your emotions, intellect, and spirituality, sparking explosive creativity. In this way, empowering your mind can break the boundaries of what confines your imagination. By understanding the yin and yang of the conscious and subconscious, you can become vastly more powerful than any supercomputer.

Understanding the natural ebb and flow of the human creative cycle can engender truly imaginative epiphanies that elevate you beyond your current constraints. Discovering your innate potential will allow you to tune into the wavelength of creativity, navigating problems and pleasure without fear.
Be bold and courageously free your mind.

Discovering and connecting to your passion may be the most powerful part of unleashing and empowering your creative spirit.

Passion process - The process of utilizing one's passion to fuel creative problem-solving techniques, connecting intellect, emotion, and spirit

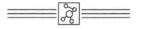

Passion connects thought processes and harnesses all aspects of the brain, enabling them to become aware of potential opportunities. Passion for a subject, concept, or dream is an incredible driving force in creativity inertia.

Creativity inertia - A powerful, dynamic, fast-paced force of creativity that does not abate no matter how great the challenge or immensity of the problem you are solving is

Ignite and set in motion heightened emotions in order to connect with your passionate desire, hope, love, and even anger. This will result in powerful intensity that can spark explosive creativity inertia.

Dynamic and passionate creativity inertia enables you to roll over challenges like a bulldozer traveling at the 200-mph speed of a Ferrari.

Creativity inertia is the ability to dynamically keep moving through problems and solving them with a high level of energy.

Our creative cycles need to be accepted as forces with a natural ebb and flow that do not inhibit creativity inertia; conversely, they allow it to become even stronger.

It is easy to misinterpret the rest cycle of creativity inertia as depression or slowed progress. In actuality, it is a powerful slingshot revitalizing you with the energy you need to explosively ascend to newfound levels of creativity.

When one is at rest, creativity inertia can be
like a whirling wheel unengaged consciously
but spinning furiously in the subconscious.
Energy is available if one can engage
the subconscious like a stick shift in a car
with the clutch pushed in
and the engine revving.
Simply pop the clutch and lay scratch to
accelerate into a conscious high-energy state.
The impassioned inventor can easily
pop the clutch of creativity inertia,
freeing the mind and igniting the imagination.

The chaos of creativity can crush us all. It is essential to learn how to successfully get in and out of the creative chaos with only what you need.

The chaos of creativity is a primordial paradise of imagination where new ideas are free to form. There is a certain freedom existing in the random, unpredictable disorder of creativity that creates constructs of unlimited imaginative potential.

Conquering the Chaos of Creativity is a construct that was created to allow you to navigate your way in a beautiful place of freedom and disorder where anything is possible. It is an imaginative mechanism I have generated in the creative chaos.

The creative chaos is a beautiful warm, blue ocean containing magnificent jewels of imagination. All you must do is dive in and get them.

The chaos of creativity is a place that has always beckoned to me, though in the past, it has also been a scary process in which I have been lost in thought. After decades of exploration, I now consider this creative chaos to be my Zen—my most familiar, fun place to navigate and to create within.

The holistic foundations of *Conquering the Chaos of Creativity* create a new dialectic of cultural language—one of creativity-based awareness, soulful communication, and revolutionary discovery.

Conquering the Chaos of Creativity is a new means of communication that transcends our linguistic constructs. By breaking the cultural boundaries that are a matrix of mental confinement, you are empowered with visionary awareness, imaginative insight, and new dreams of creative freedom.

Methodical intuition - A predictive imaginative process whereby methodical logic and intuition creatively combine to form a problem-solving construct

When you learn the process of methodical intuition and use it to harness your innate imagination, your best guess can become a scientific process of success.
Methodical intuition develops a creative construct that allows your mind to intuitively process complex information, easily arriving at a solution.

Methodical intuition is an art that can be practiced and learned. It is a personalized creative construct that can be applied to any problem or challenge.

Methodical intuition is a brilliant beacon of perception—a sacred gift that can be used to unlock your imagination.

Subconscious cloud - The process of consciously and diligently studying problem statements and pattern structures that culminates in the subconscious mind automatically yielding solutions just like a supercomputer

When you focus on finding creative solutions every minute of every day, a miraculous creative construct called the subconscious cloud is formed.

Imagining a new idea is the profound creative gesture of life.

The subconscious cloud constructs seemingly impossible puzzle pieces in an apparently automatic way.

By consciously creating imaginative problem statements, you direct the subconscious cloud, enabling the power of creativity.

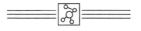

The subconscious cloud has a lofty vantage point high above the other creativity processes. It engages and energizes them in the subconscious collective of creativity.

The process of creativity sleep & dream training is an undiscovered source of creative problem-solving power that, when harnessed, can manifest solutions for the most complex problems of creativity.

Your brain is a supercomputer that can process a vast amount of information while you sleep. Even more amazing is the fact that when you are asleep, your mental processes accelerate up to six times faster than they do when you are awake.

The partnership between your conscious direction and creativity sleep stimulates imagination, clarity, and visionary dreams.

Creativity is a process of circling back to the start and beginning again. You will get closer to the solution with each revolution of imaginative focus.

An experienced guide can lead you out of
confusion using the totality of logic,
inspiration, philosophy, psychology,
and imaginative inspiration.

Confusion can be an open door leading to the
next solution. By following the footprints of
creative clues on your journey, you can ignite
your intuitive problem-solving process,
finding a new path to the solution.

A superficial problem statement is a desert mirage of creativity. The mirage seems to promise an oasis paradise in the blistering heat of problem-solving but is proven an illusion as you draw closer. This mirage quickly evaporates as you try to approach a solution.

The six foundations of *Conquering the Chaos of Creativity* give you the tools you need to unlock your imagination, allowing you to get started, achieve clarity, and free your mind. Take the first step now with confidence and courage. You will find your way.

Spiritual &
Philosophical
Creativity

A nything that is a human concern is a
spiritual concern, expressed in the syntax
of philosophy. This exquisitely impassioned
enlightenment is the soul's language, carving
cavernous reach with the deepest eddies of
your truest self.

Your inspired spirit can break you free of
whatever problems or constraints are holding
you back. Trust in the belief that you can
connect to these transcendent forces residing
deep within you and spiritually beyond you.

Reach beyond your limitations to pursue the
greater truth of your calling. The philosophy of
inspiration and empowered imagination
enlightens your spirit and soul, allowing you to
truly believe in your potential.

Intense exercise can physiologically engage the trifecta of body-mind-spirit, yielding heightened cognition, powerful imagination, and creative clarity.

Aerobic exercise gets the heart pumping and improves the function of the hippocampus, the part of the brain responsible for verbal memory and learning. In this sense, physical activity is gasoline in the engine of creative thinking.

Exercise enhances cognition through increased blood pressure and blood flow in the brain, creating more oxygen and greater mental energy.

You are special and divine—a powerful force capable of transcending your known human capacity.

Clear your mind and connect with your spiritual creativity.

Creativity meditation - An important mental, philosophical, and spiritual journey into a powerful force of imagination, inventive energy, and mental intuition

Creativity meditation is an incredibly important mental, philosophical, and spiritual journey into imagination, inventive energy, and intuition.

Every day that I design and create a new invention is, in essence, a prayer. I yearn to be able to reach further, deeper, and higher, transcending my abilities. My prayer is a wish to create inventions that are worthy and that make a difference in improving people's lives.

Your belief and faith are the weapons that most empower you in your battle to conquer the chaos of creativity.

Prayer is the connection to your highest creative power. It is a beacon of positivity and hope—a belief that out of the creative chaos of despair will come greatness, innovation, and truth.

There can be failure after failure. When one is physically and emotionally exhausted, it can seem impossible to continue. The act of never giving up and persevering in creative problem-solving may be the only thing that can pull you through.

You must continue. You must survive. Only through sheer willpower can this be done. Giving up is worse than anything else. You must be willing to sacrifice and commit all your energy to your efforts.

Touching the fire of creativity burns a hole in your soul, but you must keep moving forward, passionately inventing.

I believe the only way to persevere is to care so much about something that you find your exhaustion, pain, depression, and difficulty are really quite trivial. My key message is that you must care and believe.

We are all capable of extraordinary things, and true greatness is born by conquering the chaos of problem-solving. You must believe you can transform your struggles into opportunities for imaginative growth.

You must focus on your passionate intent in order to persevere. Passion will give you the confidence you need to be a risk-taker and to face your problems head-on. This powerful belief can overcome all obstacles you are faced with, causing them to explode with creative dynamite.

I have been in the dark place of failure many times and have learned how to never become trapped in it. Passage from imprisonment to freedom is a brief walk through an open door that is always unlocked in your transition to success.

Creative courage is the empowering force in your soul that shields your imagination from the intoxication of success and the depression of failure. Courageously undertake your idealistic journey to energetically master creative problem-solving.

Failure and success are part of the natural cycle of creative problem-solving. The powerful inventor in you must be strong to dwell in these extremes.

Each small advancement is an important artform that leads to success. By focusing on and appreciating the traversing of creativity and imagination, you ascend with creative, dynamic energy regardless of how daunting the climb may be.

In the natural cycle of creative progression, there is no failure or success; there is just the symbiotic bond between two elements that nurtures the natural process of creative evolution. Success and failure are trivial views of the greater journey of creative evolution.

The incredible sensitivity of creative power is the awareness of all possible thoughts, encompassing the complexities and patterns of your evolving concepts.

I learned how to come close to the fire of creativity without getting burned. I survived without being crushed by creativity. With awareness of the incredible sensitivity of creative power, I now fearlessly dance upon the flames.

Fragile sensitivity strengthens your thoughts and projects creativity into the problem-solving process. The incredible gift of sensitivity has immense power. It is the energy of revolutionary change and imagination.

Imagination Creativity

Believe that you can transform your dreams into reality using the guiding light of self-discovery that imagination offers. Regardless of whatever life has shaped you into up until this time, this can now be a departure point for the renewal of your soul. You can break the mold that contains you with the chisel of your energized imagination.

Imagination is your very essence as a human being. The realm of imagination is a toolbox containing wonders of creative problem-solving that can set you free from the stasis of boredom and the depression of perceived defeat. Embrace the regenerative powers your imagination offers you. It is a superpowered wellspring that energizes your dreams, enabling them to come true. Enact your will, break free, and imagine more.
Use these quotes to get started.

Lift yourself up and persevere; the barriers to creativity will crumble.

Fight daily to bend the reality of the world to embrace the evolution of your invention.

Freed from constraint, immerse yourself fully in your imagination. Believe completely in your quest and boldly dive deeper in your inquiry to find truth.

Each creative foundation of *Conquering the Chaos of Creativity* involves well-honed tools of creative problem-solving created in the four decades of my passionate pursuit of truth. It is now time for you to use these foundational tools of analytics, inspiration, psychology, philosophy & spirituality, invention, and imagination creativity to actualize your dreams.

Your mind can be your greatest imaginative invention. Set your imagination free; there are no boundaries, and there are no limits.

The personal liberation of greater imagination will set your mind free.

Conquering the Chaos of Creativity is about the moment you build organization in the freedom of creative chaos, which is an imaginative and powerfully inspirational problem-solving force. You experience a form of rebirth in which you become the truest and greatest invention. Free your mind and imagination to find your truth.

Imagination empowers your mind, body, and spirit, inspiring you to fearlessly jump off the cliff of creativity with confidence.

You are capable of transforming your dreams into reality, using the guiding light of self-discovery to imagine more.

The initial sparks of imagination exploration
are your soul breaking free from the invisible
cage of cultural constraints.

Life has molded you into what you are, but you
don't need to remain that way. By imagining
more, you can break the mold
and set yourself free.

Invention Creativity

Your greatest invention will always be yourself. Inventing is a process of revitalizing your mind, body, and spirit to create revolutionary change in the world. Within the realm of invention creativity are principles that can direct your awareness to help you achieve your goals, no matter what they may be.

The invention creativity process is a navigational compass that always points to the true north of your idealism, passion, and self-fulfillment. This ingenious revelation is the harnessing and illumination of your personal intrinsic creativity; it enables you to embrace the ultimate dream of fulfillment that may lie outside your current vision. Believe that it is there, waiting, and use the inventive spirit of your mind as the wind beneath your wings.

Creativity compass - A philosophical navigation tool that will always point to the true north of the solution you're trying to find

The creativity compass is a revolutionary construct that gives you the awareness required to find the solutions you need to achieve your goals in the creative chaos.

Wielding the creativity compass requires you to be aware, alert, and free from distractions. It is important to be introspective, constantly monitoring your clarity of thought. This will allow you to maintain balance as you innovate.

An invention is, by its very nature, interdisciplinary. Along the path that extends from concept to final solution, an inventor must learn to speak the many languages of science, business, design, and engineering.

Speak the many languages of invention to serve as a translator for brilliant people and their diverse disciplines in the process of creative invention.

Always approach a problem statement with
consideration of how information should be
translated to all stakeholders' personal
languages of invention. Incredibly innovative
concepts will almost never come from a
group of bewildered people
who do not communicate well.
They will typically arrive at a comfortable
decision that is highly flawed.
The visual vocabulary is an innovative creative
language construct that can be used to create
three-dimensional forms in design,
art, and science.

Only by deconstructing a form using visual knowledge of its primary components and geometries can we truly understand it.

Something wondrous happens when you design forms that flow from the act of improvisation. This miraculous act is derived from a well-understood and comprehensive visual vocabulary of your own design.

There must be a clear and present design theme or message that binds forms together. The resulting design must have clarity and visual purpose.

Innovative creationists strive for revolutionary new images that evoke a powerful emotional response. These images inspire a continuing fascination with form, rhythm, and harmony.

Minimalism must harness a powerful concept and extricate the essence of the idea.
This is a fundamental process that achieves revolutionary creativity.

Minimalistic essence is a form stripped bare that reveals the intrinsic beauty of elegant simplicity.

Minimalists humbly listen to a design, seeking
true substance and its essence in discovering
the most valuable qualities of
the form's minimalism.

By looking far into the future, you create a
unique problem-solving tool. This frees your
mind, allowing you to imagine a boundless
new environment.

Envision how technology can embrace our
classical human needs and manifest
true happiness.

Nature's inspiration is the genesis of ingenious
revelation and the illumination of
our intrinsic creativity.

Organic problem-solving is the process of
adapting invention, art, and science to the
revelations of our natural environment
and human needs.

In nature problem-solving, technology
surrenders and adapts to the form and
psychology of mankind. This is a prime
directive that creates imaginative solutions for
human-scale invention.

The greatest rewards of reaching the pinnacle
of the mountain in the arduous climb of
problem-solving are the clarity and
vision of creativity.

The combined optics of many disciplines form
a telescope that allows you to clearly see the
distant revelation of your visionary idea.

Build the dreams that your vision has
imagined. Re-envision the world, reawakening
your creative insight.

Analytical Creativity

In Search of
the Problem Statement

Searching for the most aware and comprehensive compendium of all one's questions is a most noble gesture of imagination. It represents passionate devotion to creative clarity, involving all of one's intellect, spirit, and courageous emotion. It is the foundation upon which a solution can be built, serving as a guiding compass that yields the answer to all your questions.

Analytical creativity is a yin and yang construct that brings order to chaos, offering the opportunity for positive change. Chaos and order are indeed the crossroads of creativity that can be navigated with total problem awareness.

In this fountainhead of awareness, the solution is already present and accessible. It enables the discovery of solutions inherent in the idealistic dreams of your life and the world at large.

Problem statement - The foundation of creative problem-solving that is built on a process of asking diverse questions about everything, then organizing a researched interacting system of creativity that contains the path to the solution

Creativity gravity is a state of mind.

Free your solution from the prison of confusion with a comprehensive and aware problem statement.

The problem statement is the master plan and foundation of creativity.

The transformation of chaos into clarity is the perpetual process of creativity.

There are devastating problems that can seemingly never be overcome. However, the solution is hidden within this conundrum; it can be discovered with a great problem statement that calls everything into question.

Free your mind from the chaos. By questioning
everything, you transform a problem into a
solution with the beautiful liberation
of creative clarity.

*Problem awareness - Awareness of the entirety
of the problem; complete understanding of all
issues, connections, and relationships.
This involves being aware of all aspects of the
problem being solved. Said awareness is based
on an understanding of many detailed
problems that culminates in complete
problem awareness.*

Developing problem awareness is a process of
continuous exploration and refinement that
frees your imagination, allowing you to
discover the true heart of the problem.

Evolving a greater understanding of the true
nature of the problem is a transformational
process that reveals the hidden
soul of creativity.

Your purposeful philosophy regarding why
the problem must be solved is empowered and
focused when you explore every detail of your
problem statement and question everything.

Creativity must be defined not only by the
solutions you create, but also by the
imaginative questions you ask.

My guiding light of creative innovation was to inspire Apple philosophically. My goal was to affect the future of humanity by embracing our idealized needs as people uncompromised and elevated by computer interaction.

Creativity gravity - A universal force that compels and attracts the dust of your beginning ideas, causing them to form an imaginative planet of thought. When you become aware of and harness the fundamental essence of this attractive force, the gravity of powerful ideas coalesces revolutionary, original thoughts.

Creativity gravity can attract and connect so many new ideas to your evolving construct that a revolution can take place, transforming your creative perspective.

There is an inexorable connection within the duality of the creative self and creative idea. It symbiotically influences a wondrous awakening of imagination.

All ideas and questions have some measure of
creativity gravity. It's universal.

There needs to be a visionary guide and leader
who can conquer the creative chaos in the
evolution of group problem-solving.

When there is an inspirational dream involving
a revolutionary creation, you must progress
with boldness and courage, believing the
magic of this vision will have the power
to be realized.

The goal is to find common ground in diverse
viewpoints, producing a foundation for making
the problem statement more comprehensive.

Analytical Creativity

In Search of
the Solution Statement

To arrive at the path that leads to your solution, you must have already traveled many roads to understand everything about the nature of your problem. You have created a detailed map of a new land that you can adventure into to find your buried treasure; hence, the saying that the solution is always contained in a well-defined problem is very true. However, how does one adventure into this wilderness to find the gold?

By using the tools of inspiration, psychological, philosophical & spiritual, invention, and imagination creativity, you will always find your path. The solution is already present and burgeoning with new ideas, concepts, and revelations. You will unleash hundreds of ideas and clues about where to adventure. The goal will be to choose which puzzle pieces fit together to envision your ideal solution. This is an exciting and inspiring time.

Explore & refine - In this process, one takes a multitude of explorative ideas and refines them based on how closely they reflect the problem statement, containing complete answers

The chorus of explore & refine is repeated in the symphony of problem-solving until the solution is reached in a crescendo of creativity.

Great artistry, sensitivity, and clarity are required for you to navigate to your most imaginative solution using explore & refine.

Due to our society's dysfunctional problem-solving process, we live in a world of our own muddled creation that does not contribute ease of use to our lives. Conversely, it produces frustration, confusion, and stress.

We must fight valiantly to free our minds, creatively developing and implementing amazing idealistic visions that help humanity.

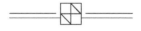

We desperately need to teach creative problem-solving, as it is the basis of our cultural salvation.

The three converging steps of explore/decide/refine funnel your imaginative thoughts, guiding them to the solution point.

The focusing of your imaginative journey liberates the final solution through each cycle of creative revolution.

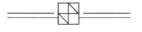

The converging steps of your imaginative journey are like a spiral wishing well. As the coin of the problem statement spins to the center, it gains momentum.

There are no walls around the human spirit, no barriers to your imagination, and no limits to what your creative vision can intuitively sense.

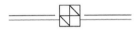

Chaos of creativity - Home for all creativity and imagination in a universe of total freedom with no boundaries. A powerful place that allows you to convene spiritual and intellectual nurturing for the genesis of revolutionary creative constructs.

The only barriers to creativity are those we erect ourselves. Let the philosophy of *Conquering the Chaos of Creativity* destroy any barriers, setting your imagination free.

Freedom of thought is a moral law of creativity. It gives soul to your philosophy, flight to your imagination, and power to your idealistic dreams. By breaking a problem down into its core simplistic elements using the building blocks of creativity, you use an intuitive process of imagination that unleashes virtually limitless ideas.

When you have fun like a child and let your imagination go wild, a vast quantity of creative opportunities will flow forth in a streaming river of creativity.

Thought molecule - A theory of problem-solving and solution formation. Ideas are like atoms and molecules, capable of being combined to form new elements and new compositions.

Applying the thought molecule concept to complexity generates creative constructionist clarity.

The intimate awareness and mastery of how thoughts combine to form transformative revolutionary concepts is the natural life-giving process of creativity.

When a creative and imaginative
problem-solving mechanism is mindfully
established, solutions instantly begin
to present themselves.

I now realize my most valuable lesson:
creativity is a state of mind that, when attained,
energizes and focuses your imagination,
allowing you to intuitively solve any problem.
This state of mind elevates your imagination
above the facts and figures
that limit your creativity.

Intuitively projecting puzzle piece concepts
that you create into a new imagined vision is
the intrinsic nature of creativity.

The intellectual bravery needed to contend
with chaos and one's yearning to depart from
an existing construct form the syntax
of creative evolution.

By observing every clue of creativity, you can
find the solution hidden within the most
mysterious and complex of problems.

A problem is essentially a crime scene with
clues that, when amassed into an accurate
theory, give you an understanding of the
true nature of the solution.

Scrutinize every detail for clues you can use to
recreate the creative crime scene.
Understanding the true nature of a problem is
the start of finding a solution.

A state of mind that embodies a keen sense of
awareness is essential in the process
of creative problem-solving.

The regenerative essence of creativity can
renew one's spirit and life.

At its core, creative problem-solving has
symbiotic yin & yang connectivity. A great
problem statement contains the solution, and
an ideal solution is generated using a
problem statement with awareness.

Conclusion

Willingness to expand your sense of self and bravely explore ideas will reveal the truth of your greatest creative potential.
The revolutionary power of inspiration that can break down all barriers to creativity is awaiting your embrace. It is time to break free of what has imprisoned your creative mind and to realize your true potential.

Now is the time to ignite the spark of the creative fire that has been simmering within you for so long. Treasure the gifts of inspiration that embolden your revolutionary vision, as you may just now be feeling that you are more powerfully creative and imaginative than you were ever aware of. Every day holds the opportunity for your unbridled imaginative freedom to do inconceivably great things. The alarm clock of creativity will sound every day, calling you to be truly inspired.

Made in the USA
Middletown, DE
17 April 2023

28796942R00057